Introduction

This manual has been designed as a guide to help you through the preliminary stages of musical theory. It includes guides to time signatures, notes and basic musical terms.

The first thing to remember about all musical theory is not to panic. All music is logical and there are very few situations where a logical solution will not present its self. The second thing to remember is that music is a language with its own rules of punctuation and grammar, just like English and if you obey those rules you won't go far wrong.

In this newly revised version of a classic book I've tried to include some new ideas from my teaching and experience to make things even easier!

J Knight. 2024.

Chapters

Chapter 1 (Pitch and the Stave) 2 - 5
Chapter 2 (Simple Time) 6 - 12
Chapter 3 (Semitones and Key Signatures) 13 - 15
Chapter 4 (The Difference between major and Minor) 19 - 19
Chapter 5 (Compound Time *Introduction*) 20 – 21

APPENDIX: Musical Terms

Chapter 1 (Pitch and the Stave)

Let's start with the basics of music, the notes. They sit on what we call the stave. On the stave you will always find a clef, this shows us at what pitch the music lies. For example the bass clef lies much lower in pitch than the treble clef. There are five lines and four spaces created by the lines. A note sits on each, the higher a note lies on the stave the higher its pitch. We give each of these pitches a letter name. We use seven letters in total *A, B, C, D, E, F, G* and repeat them endlessly as the pitch gets higher or lower. The position of each note, and therefore its pitch, on the stave <u>never</u> changes.

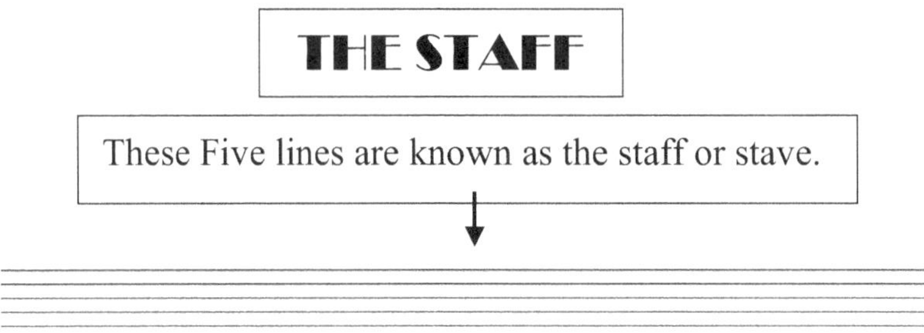

ALL OF THE NAMES OF THE NOTES

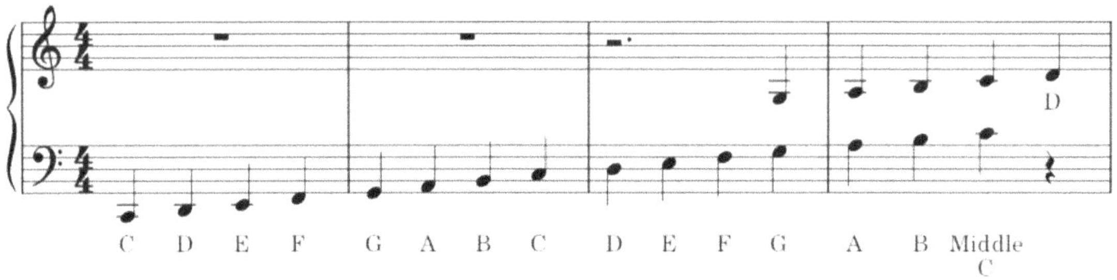

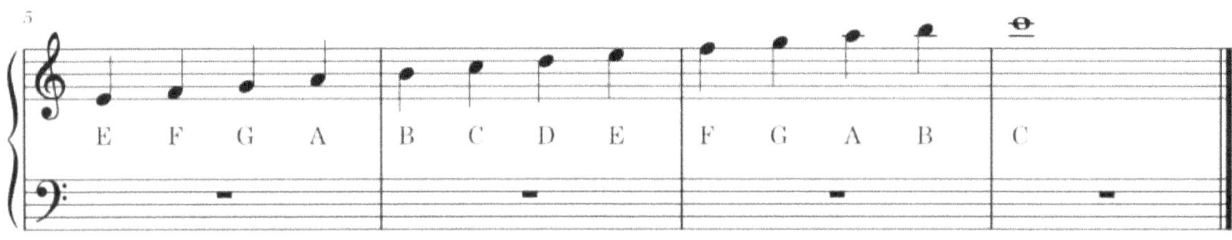

In example 1 we can see that there are some convenient rhymes that can be used to remember the position of each note on the stave.

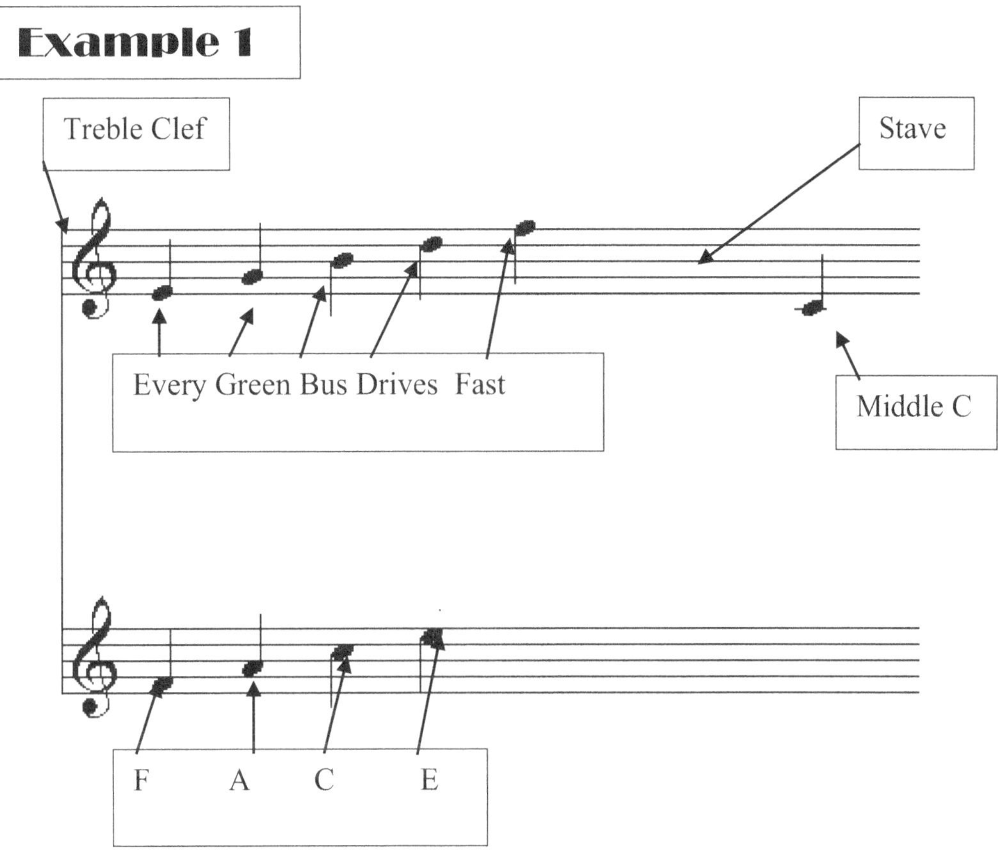

It is important to note at this point that the positions of the notes on the stave are dictated by the clef in front of it. So for the bass clef we need to learn another set of rhymes. These can be seen in example 2. If I am teaching the piano I find it helpful to tell students that it is humans with the right and animals for the left. Therefore the right hand is FACE for the spaces and Every Green Bus Drives Fast for the line and the left hand is All Cows Eat Grass and Great Big Dogs From Africa for the lines. It helps pupils not to get confused by making this differentiation.

As you can see from both examples there is a note pointed out called middle C. This note can usually be found in the middle of the piano, as its name would suggest and it serves as a vital navigation point for musical theory in that its location in each clef can give us a clear idea where the pitch lies. Example 3 shows us standard layout for every Keyboard instrument. In musical theory this can be very useful in visualising certain concepts.

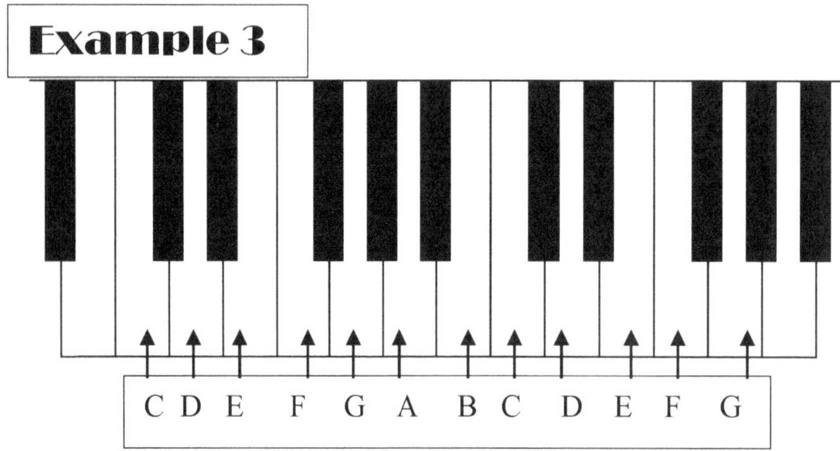

Now we have a basic way in which to find the pitches and the names of the notes on the stave lets investigate those notes that occur below the stave. These can be worked out quite logically by using the alphabet; this can be clearly seen in example 4 working step by step as the music is going down or up.

Example 4

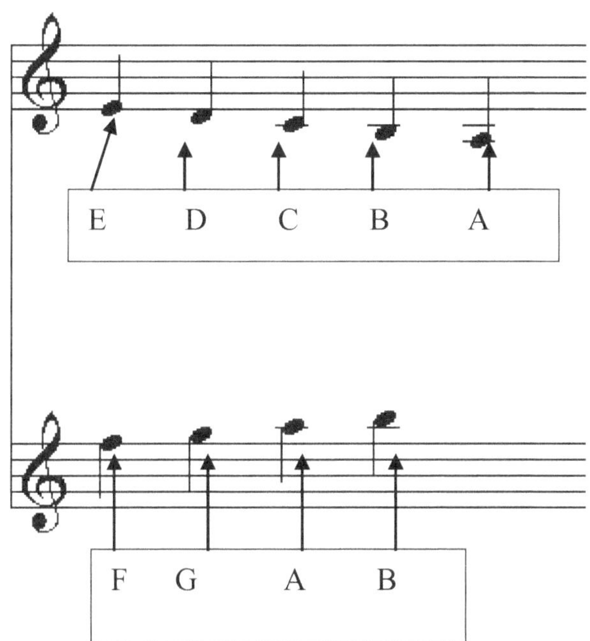

You may have noticed that for some of the notes in example 4 some funny little lines have appeared. Don't panic, these are called ledger lines. When we as musicians run out of lines on the stave we simply draw another one underneath the note. This is a very common practice and you will find it in most pieces of music.

So to conclude, we can find most notes logically by working out their relationship to middle C. They move by step alphabetically and there are rhymes that we can use to quickly find out their letter names.

Chapter 2 (Simple Time)

As musicians we have to find ways of recording time. Without time we would have no concept of beat or pulse. Every piece of music has a beat, a regular pulse of time that is worked out by the performer by the use of a metronome in divisions of a minute. So therefore if a composer stated that he wanted a piece of music to be played at 60 beats per minute those beats would work out to be exactly the same speed as the seconds hand on your watch.

As I pointed out in the introduction music has its own grammar and punctuation, just as English has. The bar and the time signature make up a significant part of this grammar. Examples of this can be seen in example 5.

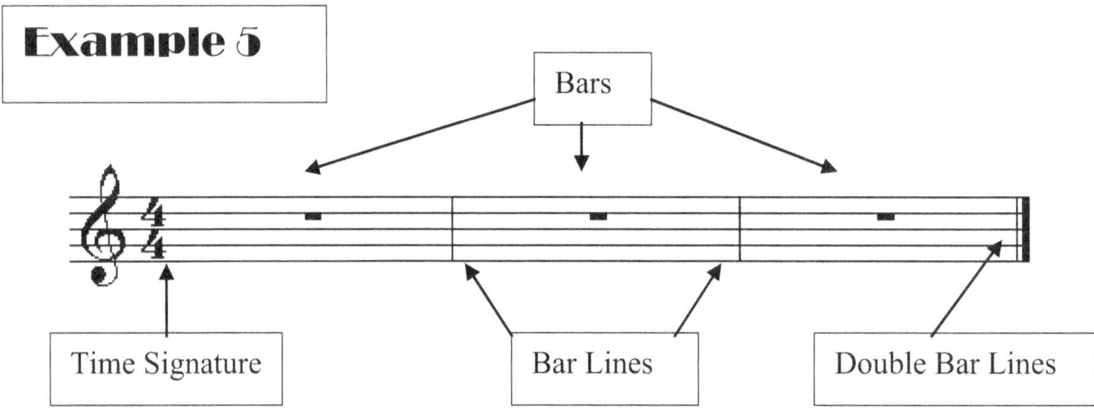

Bars and bar lines are directly related to the time signature. If you notice there are two numbers in the time signature in example 5. The top number in the time signature means the number of beats in the bar and the bottom number means the type of beats to be used in that bar.

In music we have types of notes that are all of differing lengths. This enables us to build different rhythms into the music. Some of these notes are listed in example 6. The bars are divided by bar lines. These are a single line that cuts straight through the stave. To signify the end of a piece of music we use the double bar line.

The type of beat can sometimes be a problematic area to deal with. Students often get confused as to the meaning of the bottom number in a time signature and its significance. To begin with I would like to introduce you to four different types of notes, four different ways of dividing the bar if you like. The semi-breve, the minim, the crotchet, and the quaver. These can all be clearly seen on example 6.

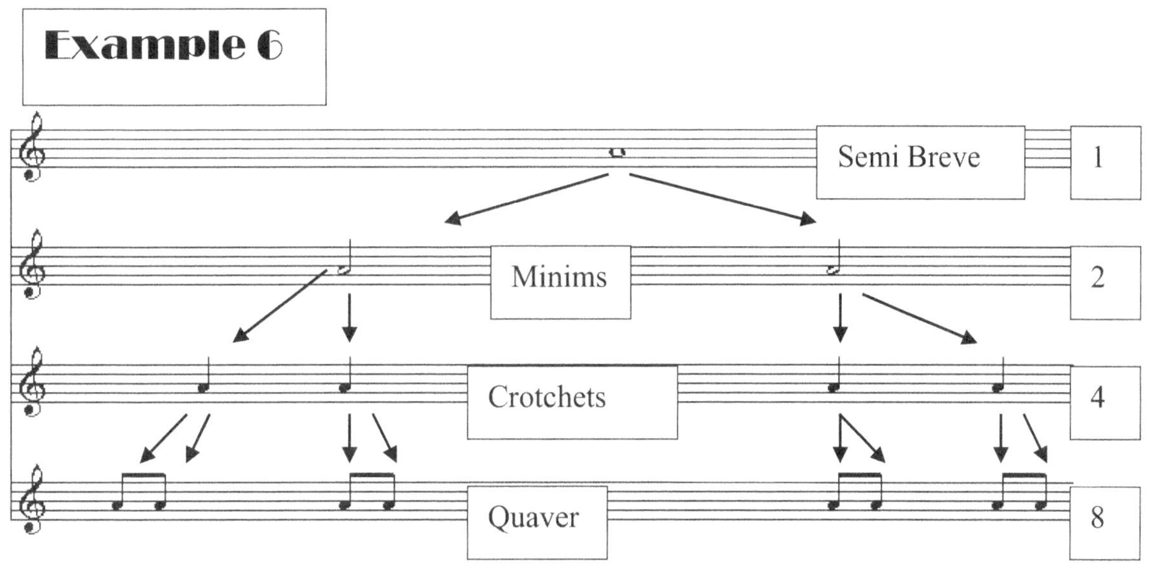

If you look at example 6 you will notice that there is a number at the end of each stave. This number indicates the quantity of that note you can get to the semi-breve and it is these divisions, which we as musicians use to define the beat. Therefore if the bottom number on a time signature were 2 you would know that the beat for that piece of music would be a minim, or if it were 4 you would know the beats would be a crotchet.

There is one very important thing to remember about bars and that is that you cannot go over the value stated in the time signature. This means that if you had a time signature, which stated that, there were four beats to the bar and those beats were crotchets you would not be able to put five crotchets in that bar.

A Simple way of working out any time signature:

As we discussed in the previous paragraphs the time signature is made up of two numbers. If you think in terms of the total number being literal i.e. the number of beats the composer wants in the bar and the second number being code. Now for any code you need to be able to decode it. In music the bottom number is easy to decode. So for example:

Example 6a

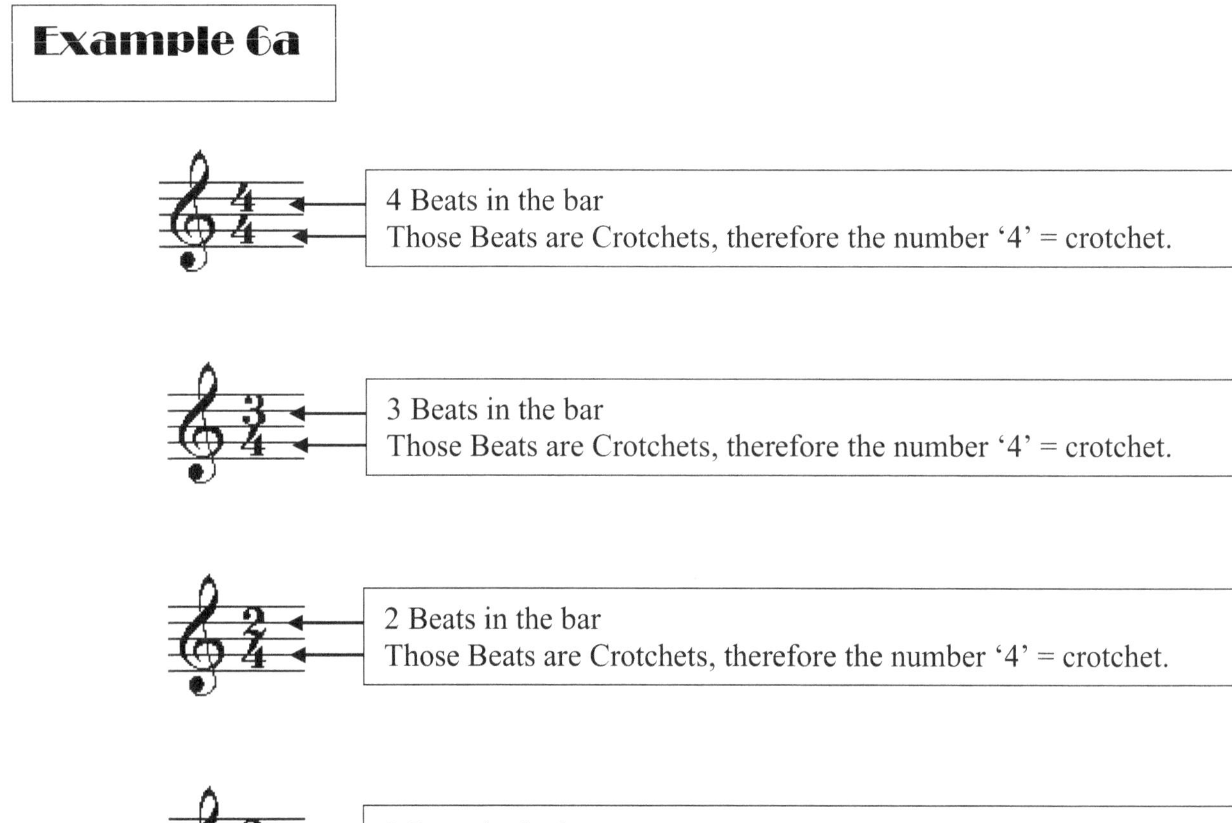

So if you're ever stuck to work out a time signature start with this method. It will always mean that you have a good basis to start. You have to also understand that there are two types of time signature, simple and compound and for a compound time signature the method needs a further step. We will deal with compound time signatures later on in this book.

A Question that some times comes up is "How many bars can you fit into a piece of music?" The answer to this is that it does not matter how many bars there are in a piece of music, you could have an infinite number.

The speed at which a piece of music is taken is determined by the metronome mark. This can usually be found at the beginning of a piece of music. An example of this can be seen in example 7.

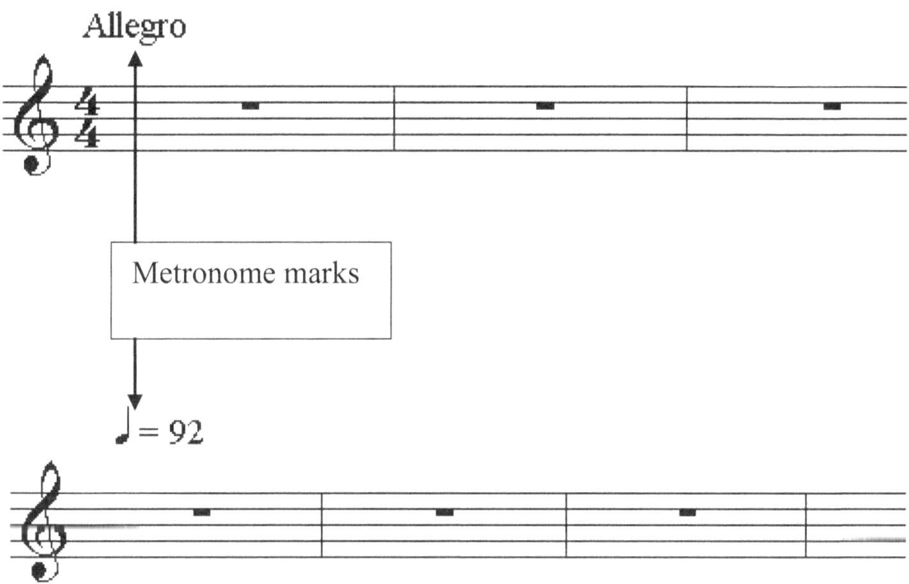

There are two different ways of writing a metronome mark. One is precise and one is quite subjective. The first is an Italian term, which means lively or brisk. The other mark means a crotchet would equal 92 beats in the minute.

There is another aspect to time in music, which is the rest. Rests are put in music at a point where the composer decides that she does not want any music to be played. They hold the same time values, as there note counterparts. Examples of rests can be seen in example 8.

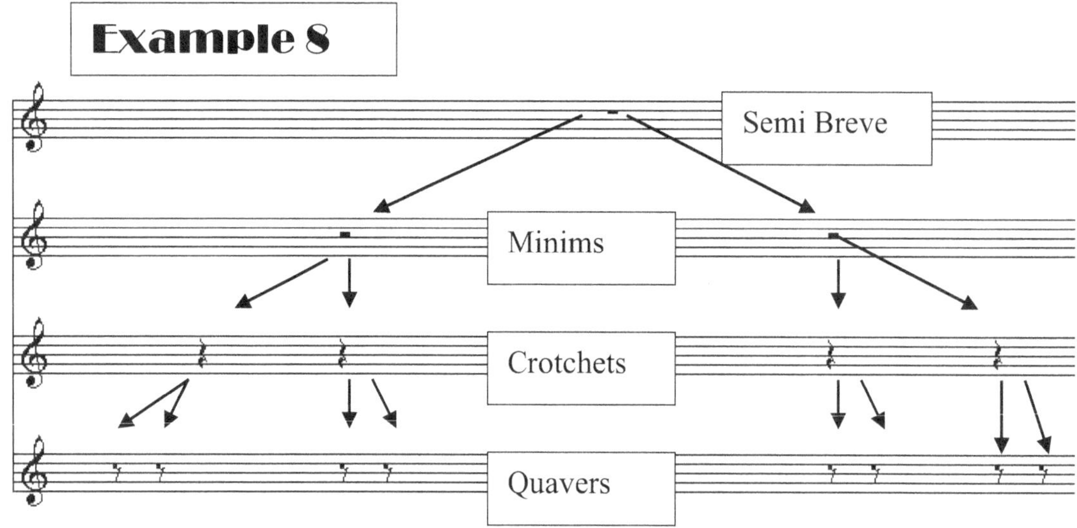

Rests can be inserted in any bar in place of a note. It has to be noted at this point that there are two different ways of writing a quaver. These can both be seen in example 9. The reason we do this is that so the musician can differentiate between a single quaver and a crotchet

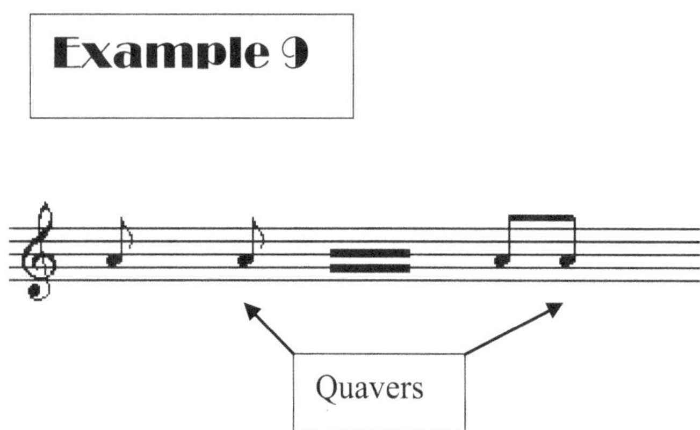

Now that we have discussed the note and the rest it is time to discuss what adding a dot to both does? Adding a dot to a note or rest adds to the value of that note. The value that the dot adds is exactly one half again. So therefore a dot added to a crotchet would make it worth three quavers instead of two, or a dot added to a minim would make it worth three crotchets instead of two. This can most clearly be seen in example 10.

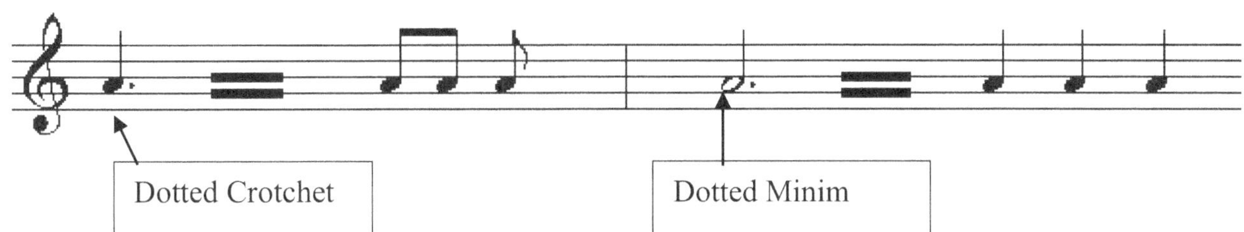

It is now important to discuss the tie. Ties occur usually when a composer wants to break the rule about only having the number of beats to the bar as specified in the time signature. Of course it is impossible to break this rule, but there is another way of achieving the same affect, the tie. If for instance you wanted to write a dotted minim and you only have two beats left in your four crotchet beats in a bar, you could tie a minim over to a crotchet. A tie joins two note values together making them larger. This can be seen in example 11.

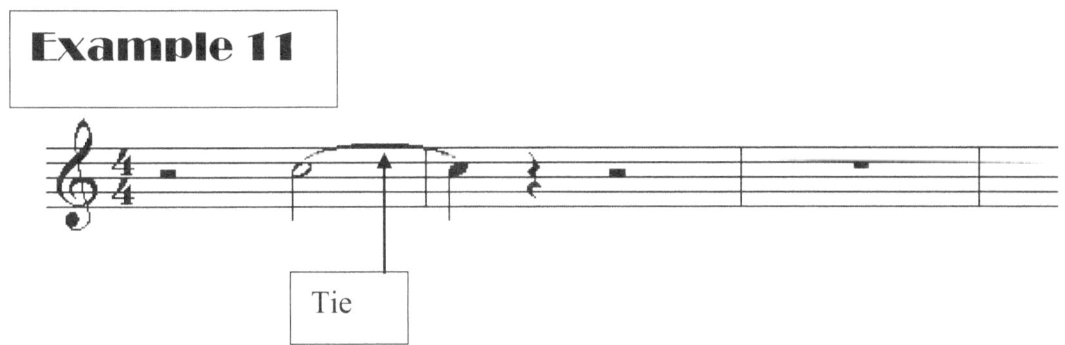

Finally in this chapter I would like to come to why I entitled this chapter "Simple Time", why not just call it time? The reason for this is that we have been investigating what is known as 'Simple Time' in the musical world. There is another sort of time called compound time. I will be discussing this in later chapters. The best way for me to leave simple time is with some examples of simple time signatures in example 12. It is also vital that I mention that there are two different ways of writing four, four and two, two, these are both explained in example 12.

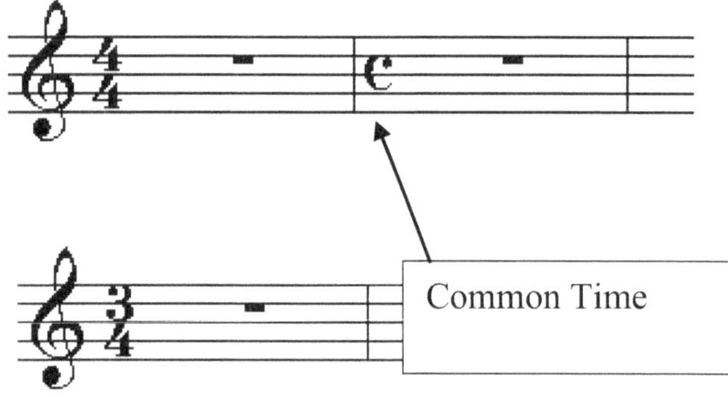

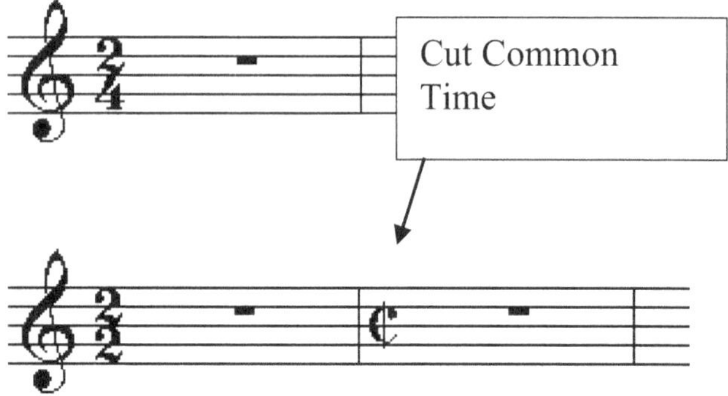

The use of common and cut common time is very common and it is vital that the student familiarise themselves with both ways of writing these.

Chapter 3 **(Semitones and key signatures)**

Now we have discussed basic time and pitch it is time to introduce a couple of difficult concepts. Semitones and Keys are most easily defined using our diagram of the keyboard. If you noticed there are black as well as white keys on the keyboard, the black keys are known as sharps and flats. They are half notes between the normal notes. We need these notes so that we can write down the major scale (we will discuss the major scale more fully later in this chapter). This can all be clearly seen in example 13.

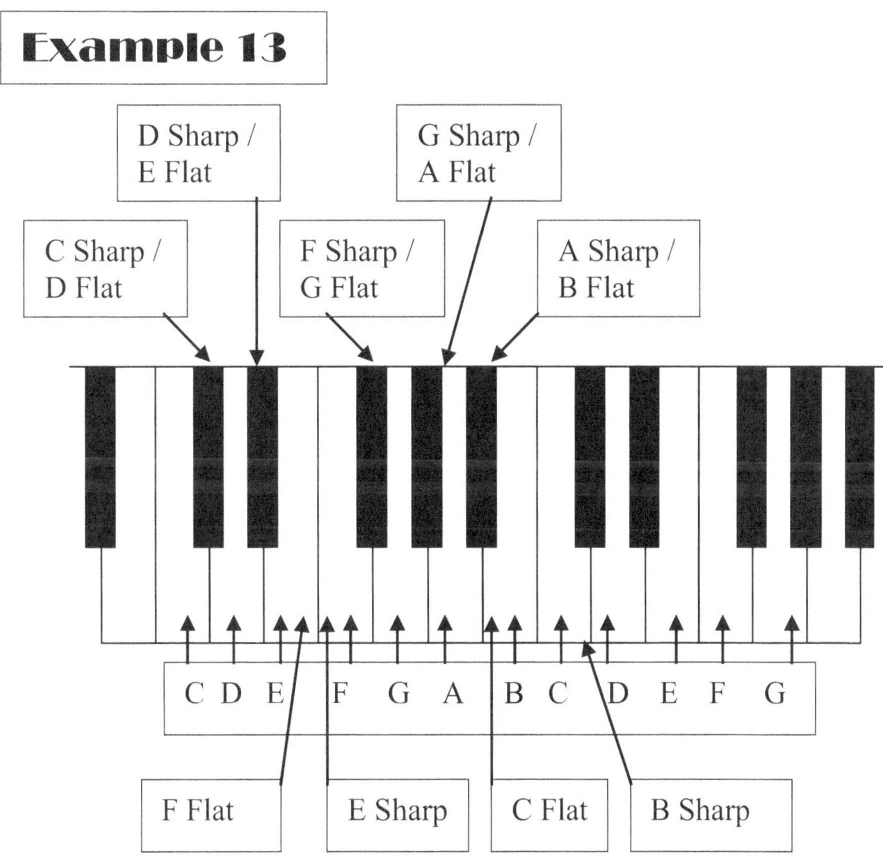

You will have noticed that each sharp or flat has two letter names and you might think this confusing, but if you remember that a sharp goes up and a flat goes down you will not go far wrong. You will also have noticed that there are four white notes that are also flats and sharps. The reason for this is that a semitone occurs between the white notes of E and F and B and C (if you notice there is no black note in-between these white notes). The letter names of the white notes are otherwise known as naturals.

Sharps and flats have their own set of rules. They do not affect the timing of a piece of music, but they do affect the pitch. They can be added to any piece of music either by the use of a key signature or by an accidental. I would like to deal with the rules that apply to the accidental first.

There is no limit to the amount of accidentals you are allowed to use in one bar, but if you do decide to use an accidental its effect only lasts for one bar. For example if a composer were to write an F sharp in one bar and then want it to repeat to the next she would have to write it again in the next bar. You have three different types of accidentals to use. The sharp, the flat, and the natural, each of these is only applicable if it does not appear in the key signature (Naturals never appear in the key signature because unless there is a sharp or flat it is always assumed that a note is natural). Examples on how to write sharps and flats can be seen in example 14.

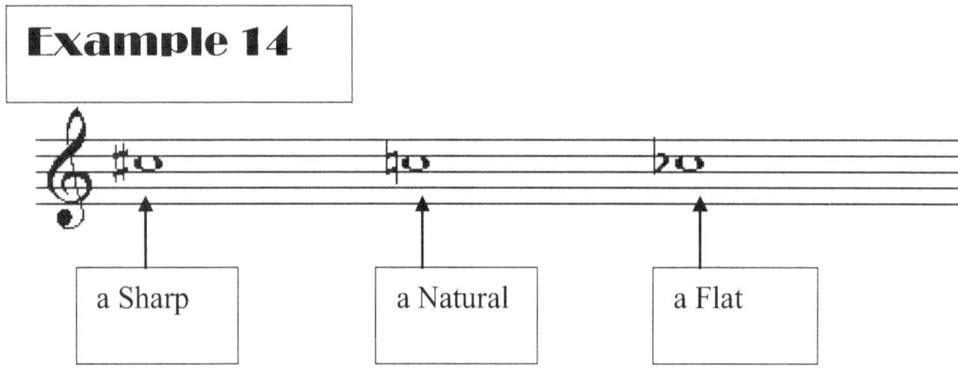

Any accidental may be cancelled out by the other. So if you were to write an A flat followed by an A sharp the A sharp would remain for the rest of that bar.

Lets now move on to the subject of keys and key signatures. The key signature is a group of sharps or flats at the beginning of a piece of music. These sharps and flats sit on a line or space on the stave telling the musician that that particular note is to be played for the whole piece of music as a sharp or flat. Now it is important to note that the sharp or flat in the key signature applies to all of the notes with that letter name, not just the ones on that line or space. For example if a composer was to put a B flat into the key signature, and we were using the treble clef, the B's below and above the stave would be flat as well. There is also something else you have to realise about key signatures and that is you cannot mix both sharps and flats in the same key signature. We also have to know that the sharps and flats that are in the key signature have to be put there in a certain order. We can find examples of key signatures in example 15. *All of the major & minor keys are in the Circle of Keys in the appendix.*

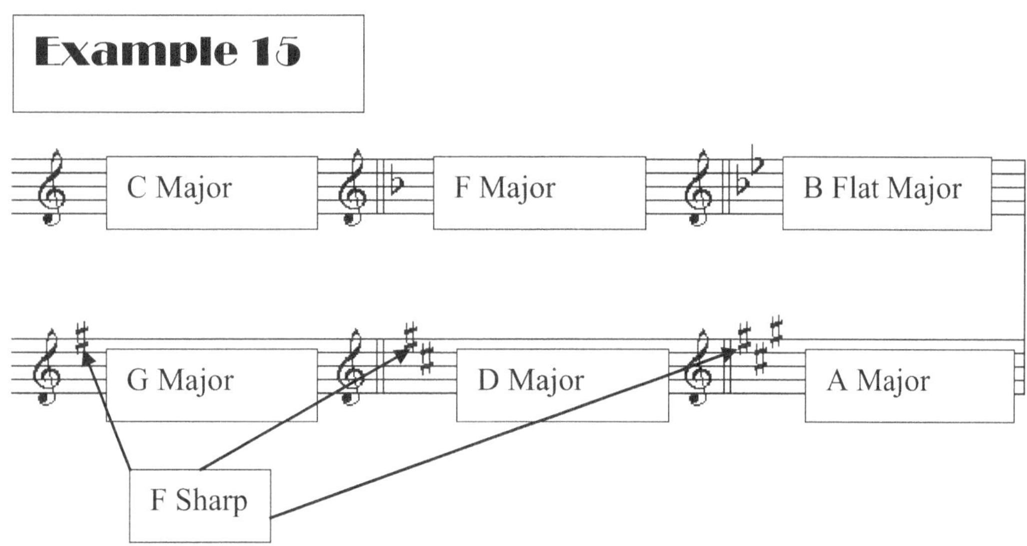

If you notice the key signatures are labelled C major, F major, B flat major etcetera, this is because each key signature has its own major and minor scale. There is another thing that you should notice about the key signatures in example 15 and that is that once a sharp or flat is added it stays in all of the subsequent key signatures. So for example if you look at the G major key signature and then the D major one and then the A major you will notice that the F sharp is present for all of them. Indeed the F sharp will be present in all sharp key signatures as will the B flat be present in all flat key signatures.

I mentioned in the previous paragraph that there was a thing called a scale and that it had two versions, the major and the minor. I would like to discuss the major scale first, as it is often the one that students will encounter first. All major and minor scales have eight notes to them and the distance between the first and last degrees of the scale is called an octave. The major scale has two semitones in it they fall in-between the 3rd and 4th and 7th and 8th degrees of the scale. Before I continue I feel that I must explain what the degrees of the scale are. We as

musicians number each note of the scale. This can be clearly
seen in example 16.

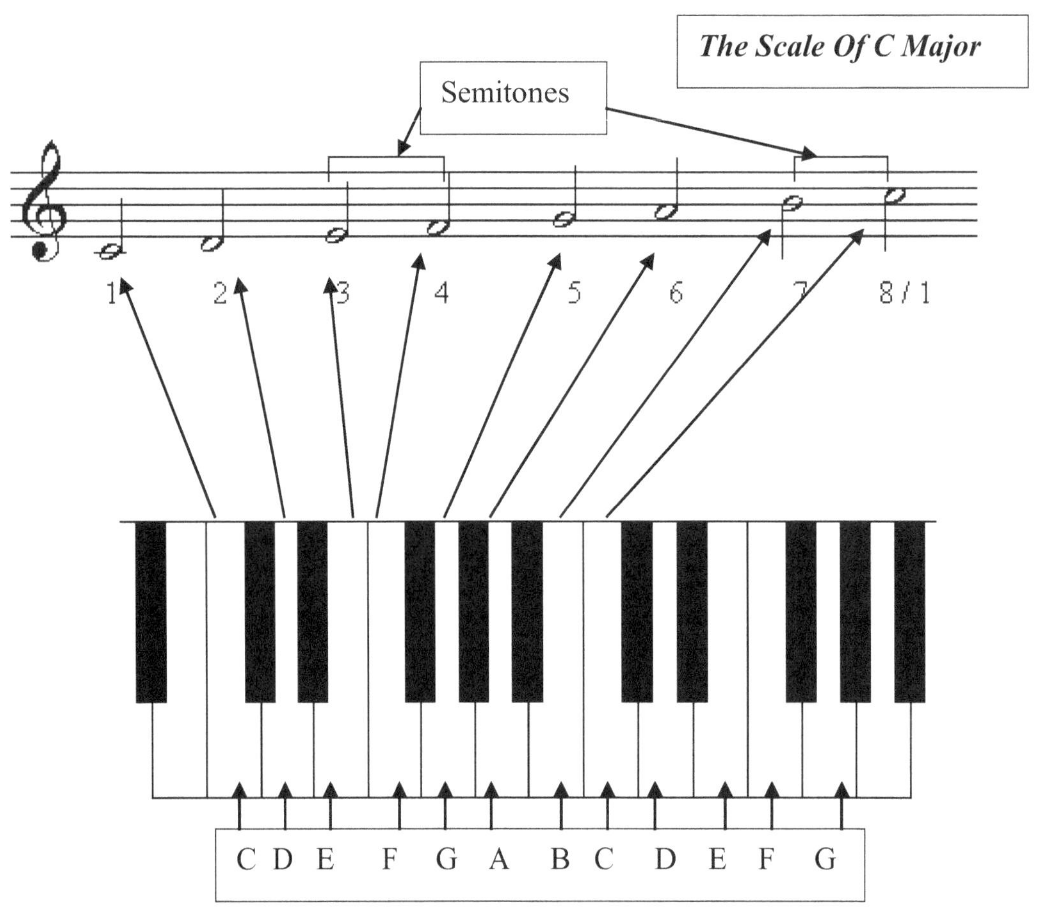

I would like to point out that the semitones in the major
scale never change their position. So they always occur on the 3rd
and 4th degrees and the 7th and 8th degrees of the scale. So
therefore taking this into account if you were to start a scale on
the note of D and continue it for the octave you would have to
introduce an F sharp and a C sharp to place the semitones
correctly.

Chapter 4 (The Difference Between Major & Minor)

We discussed in the previous chapter that there was a thing called a major scale. It has eight notes in it and that there is a set position for two semitone differences in the notes to occur. We also discussed the fact that there was a thing called a key signature, which we use in music to define the key. I also mentioned that there was a thing called a minor scale. There are two different types of minor scale, the harmonic and the melodic. Both of these scales share a relationship with the same major scale. Every major scale has a relative minor. This basically means that the two scales share a key signature.

Lets start our look at the minor scale with the minor version. You can see A harmonic minor in example 17.

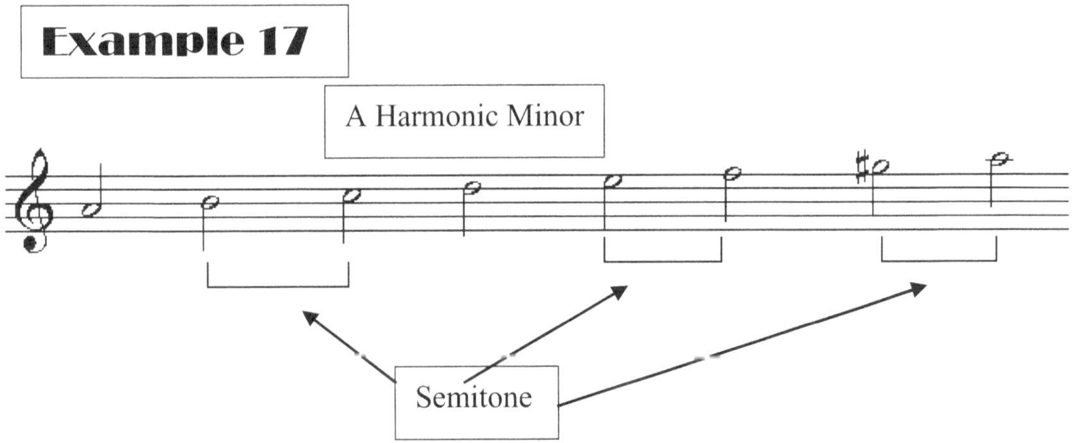

The minor scale has one very important point and that is that it is always necessary to put in some accidentals. In the harmonic minor you can clearly see that there are three semitones present rather than the major scales two. These semitones take between the 2nd and 3rd, 5th and 6th, and the 7th and 8th degrees of the scale. If you follow this model exactly you will always find that the harmonic minor scale is correct.

I would now like to quickly go over the relationship between the major and the minor scale. I have already mentioned that major and minor scales share key signatures. The question that you are now asking yourself is how do I find out this relationship? The answer to this is quite simple you count three semitones down. So therefore if I wished to find out the relative minor of F major I would count down three semitones from the keynote of F and I would arrive at the note D. Therefore the relative minor to F major is D minor and it does not matter whether the minor is harmonic or melodic.

Now lets look at the melodic minor. We have already discovered that it shares a key signature with its harmonic relative; they also obviously start on the same note, so what is the difference? Lets look at example 18.

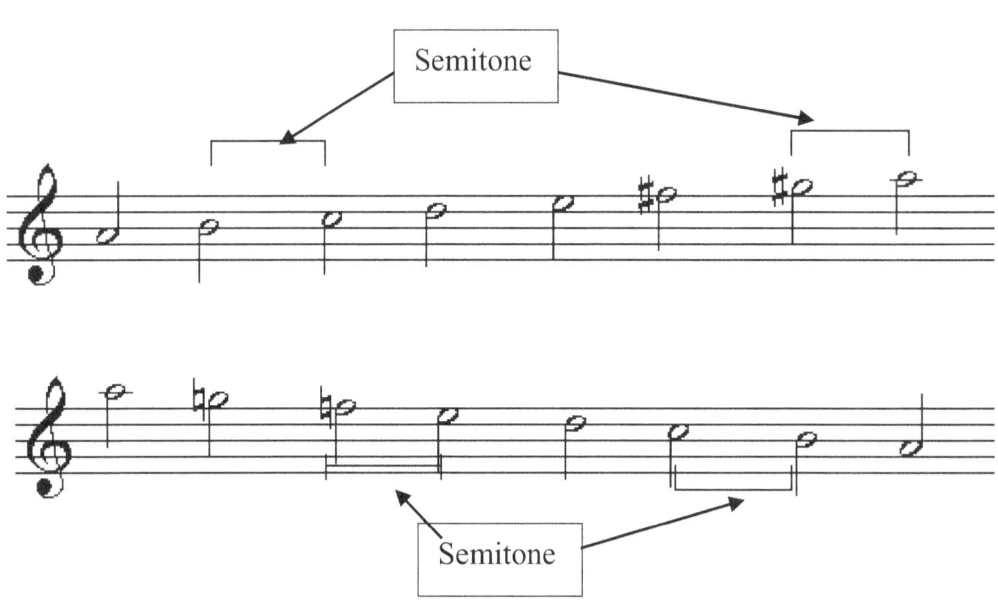

The difference lies in the semitones. As with all types of scales the position of tones and semitones defines what that scale is. As musicians we call this tonality. There are again three different semitones, but there is one major difference and that is you do not play the same notes ascending as you do descending. Ascending the semitones take place on the 2nd and 3rd, and the 7th and 8th degrees of the scale. Descending they take place on the 6th and 5th, and again between the 3rd and 2nd degrees of the scale. I have shown this difference in example 18 and I have included all of the necessary accidentals to make this possible.

I would like just to talk at this point about triads. These are not a set of eastern gangsters, but are in fact a combination of notes, which we find quite commonly in musical theory. As the name would suggest there are three notes to it. To create one it is quite simple, take the first note and then count up three, so if we take C and we count up three we would get the next not as an E, then we take our first note and count up five, in our example we get the note G. This can be seen most clearly in example 19.

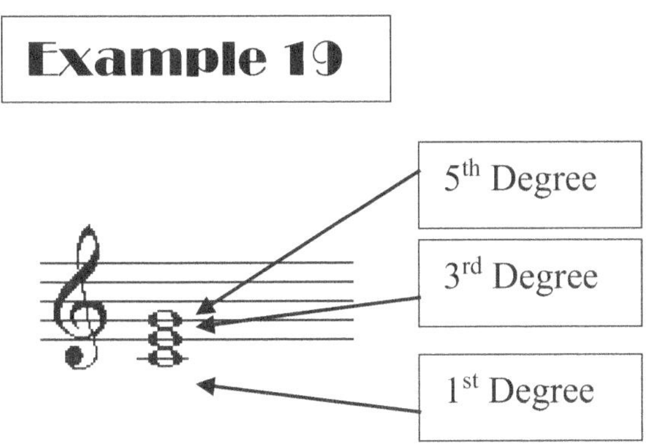

I hope that this chapter will have helped a little in showing certain aspects of major and minor. If you stick to the formulas shown you will not go far wrong.

Chapter 5 (Compound Time *Introduction*)

We have already covered simple time in chapter 2, but there are two types of time commonly used in music. In this final chapter I would like to discuss something that frequently gives students problems. In compound time we most frequently have a dotted beat. If you remember from chapter two we discussed the dotting of notes. This is a process whereby you add a dot to a note and it makes that notes half as long again. This has the effect of making the typical compound time beat a dotted crotchet that is worth three quavers. In example 20 we can see three of the most common types of compound time signatures.

Example 20

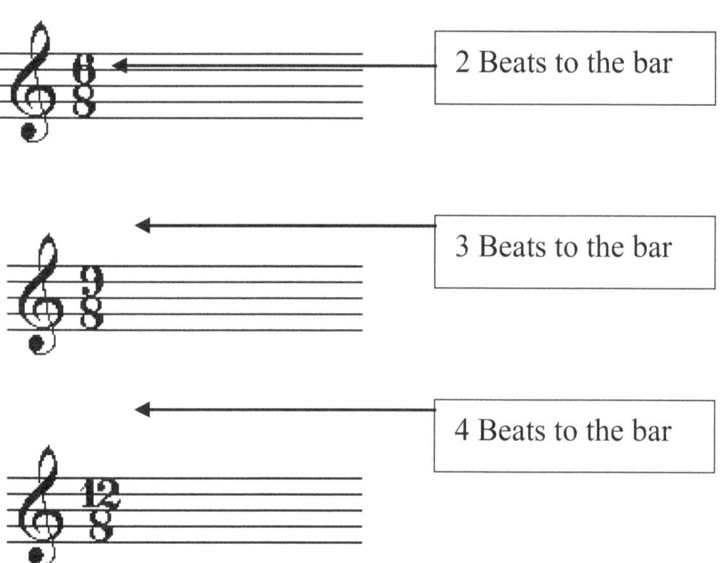

You will notice that all of the time signatures show that the beat is to be in quavers. This is most commonly not the case and you usually divide the top number by three and you will get your compound beat.

So in conclusion Compound time is quite simple if you remember that there are three quavers per beat instead of two. You must not forget that to get a correct time signature in compound time you must divide it by three.

I would just like to make a quick note on grouping of notes. This is a way of setting out music so it is easy to read. We mentioned in chapter two that quavers can be beamed together and notes can be tied to one another. This has to be applied in bars of music to show the beat more clearly, so for example if you were to take a two four bar and you wanted a quaver followed by a crotchet followed by a quaver it would be clearer for the performer for you to write four quavers and tie the middle two, that way the beat becomes clearer. I have included my four tips for note grouping.

1. Break down the piece into quavers.
2. Then sort the quavers into beats.
3. Look for <u>any</u> note that crosses a beat and then eliminate. it by the use of a tie.
4. Group all notes according to the beat.

I hope that this small book has been of use to those of you that found musical theory a previously impenetrable barrier. It has been intended to be a useful supplement and aid for musical theory.

Appendix

Term	Translation	Meaning
Tempo	*time*	The speed of music e.g. 120 BPM
Grave	*solemn*	Slow and solemn, slower than largo
Largo	*broad*	Slow and dignified
Larghetto	*a little bit broad*	Not as slow as largo
Lentando	*slowing*	Becoming slower
Lento	*slow*	Slow
Adagio	*at ease*	Slow, but not as slow as largo
Adagietto	*little adagio*	Faster than adagio; or a short adagio composition
Andante	*at a walking pace*	Moderately slow, flowing along
Andantino	*slightly faster than andante*	slightly faster than andante
Moderato	*moderately*	At a moderate speed
Allegretto	*a little bit joyful*	Slightly slower than allegro
Largamente	*broadly*	Slow and dignified
Allegro	*joyful; lively and fast*	Moderately fast
Sostenuto	*sustained*	A slowing of tempo, often accompanied by legato playing
Fermata -	*stopped*	Marks a note to be held or sustained
Presto	*ready*	Very fast
Prestissimo	*very ready*	Very *very* fast, as fast as possible
Accelerando	*accelerating*	Accelerating
Allargando	*slowing and broadening*	Slowing down and broadening, becoming more stately and majestic, possibly louder
Ritardando	*slowing down*	Decelerating
Rallentando	*becoming progressively slower*	Decelerating
Rubato	*robbed*	Free flowing and exempt from steady rhythm
Tenuto	*sustained*	Holding or sustaining a single note
Alla marcia	*as a march*	In strict tempo at a marching pace (e.g. 120 bpm)
A tempo	*to time*	Return to previous tempo
L'istesso tempo	*Same speed*	At the same speed
Crescendo	*growing*	Becoming louder
Decrescendo	*shrinking*	Becoming softer
Diminuendo	*dwindling*	Becoming softer
Marcato	*marked*	A note played forcefully
Forte - f	*strong*	Loud
Fortissimo -	*very strong*	Very loud
Mezzo Forte - mf	*half-strong*	Moderately loud
Piano -	*gentle*	Soft
Pianissimo - pp	*very gentle*	Very soft
Mezzo Piano -	*half-gentle*	Moderately soft

The Progression of Keys:

To Remember The Sharps and Flats There are Two Rhymes To Remember

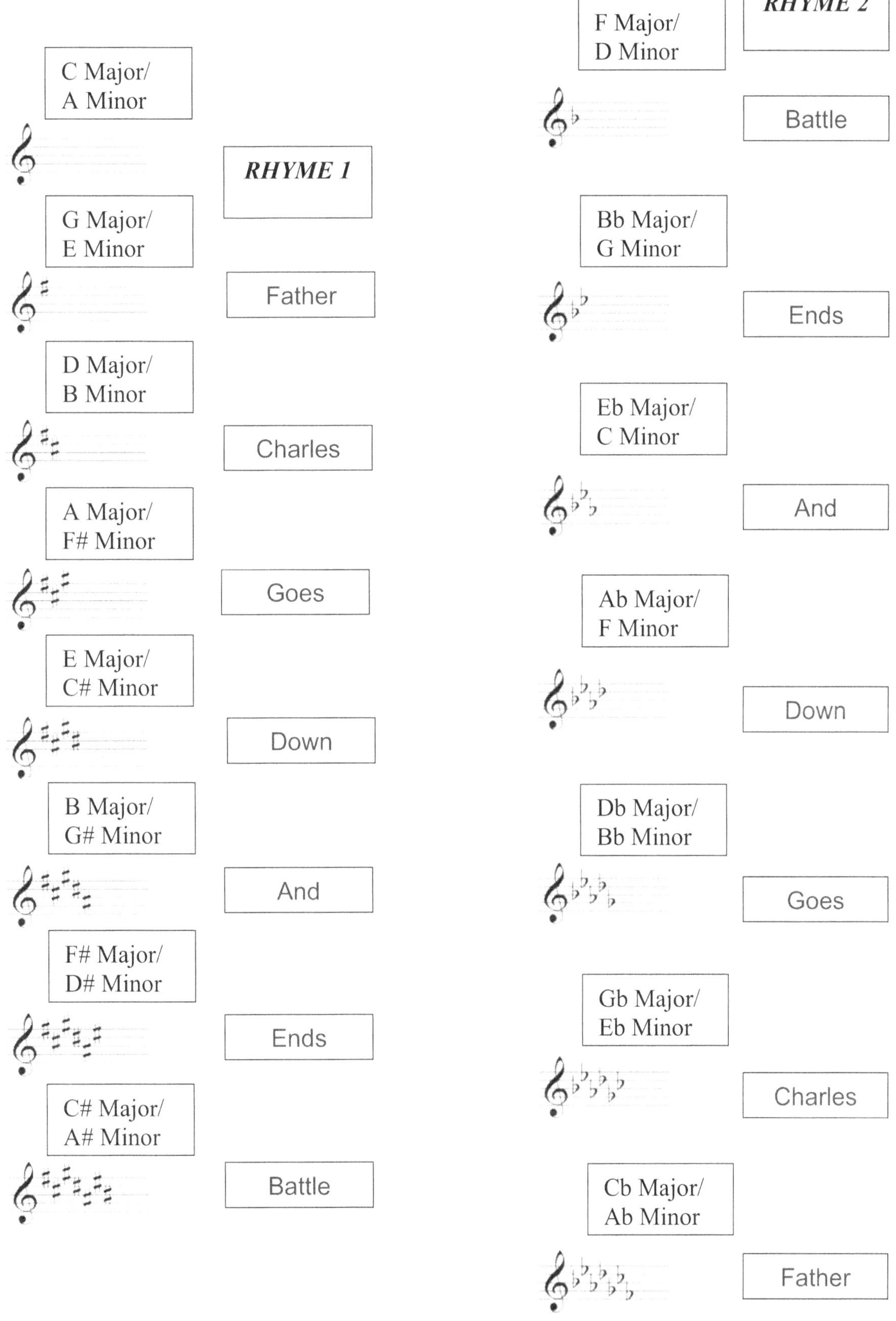

www.ingramcontent.com/pod-product-compliance
Lightning Source LLC
Chambersburg PA
CBHW080249260726
48658CB00008B/3300